Raspberry Pi For Beginners

How to get the most out of your raspberry pi, including raspberry pi basics, tips and tricks, raspberry pi projects, and more!

Table Of Contents

Introduction

I want to thank you and congratulate you for downloading the book, "Raspberry Pi For Beginners".

This book contains helpful information about getting started with using your Raspberry Pi – from the basics of this computer system, as well as the peripherals and parts you will need to assemble one.

You will learn about the different Raspberry Pi's available, and the differences between each. No matter which version of the Pi you have, this book will help you to use it successfully.

Covered in this book are the different uses of the Pi, projects you can undertake, capabilities of the Pi, and some handy Pi hacks that will make using the Raspberry Pi a lot easier!

This book will explain to you tips and techniques that will allow you to begin successfully understanding, using, and getting more out of your Raspberry Pi today!

Thanks again for downloading this book. I hope you enjoy it!

Chapter 1:
What is a Raspberry Pi?

A petite, fundamental computer, the Raspberry Pi is fast gaining popularity among students, teachers and computer enthusiasts. Built by a UK charity, the Pi is a very useful and capable low-cost device with a very tasteful name. It can be plugged into a TV or computer monitor and it utilizes a typical keyboard and mouse. It functions like your regular desktop computer – word processing, making spreadsheets, playing games, playing hi-def videos, completing electronics projects, and browsing the Internet.

The main objective of the foundation was to develop an affordable computer with free software that can be used by students. This will cultivate interest in learning about computers, computer science and technology. It is a solitary-board computer embossed with connectors and chips and runs on three Linux-based OS. Developers have been working to provide an educational edition Raspberry Pi which will come with pre-loaded software and documentation.

The Pi can be used by anyone to explore computing. It can also be employed in programming languages such as Python and Scratch. Children can learn to program codes and get a better understanding of how computers and technology work.

The earliest Raspberry Pi or RPi has the following specifications:

- The system-embedded chip or SoC is a Broadcom BCM2835.

- Contains ARM1176JZFS processor

- Runs at 700MHz

- GPU Video Core 4 (capable graphics core, has BluRay quality playback; capable of hardware decoding with H.264 codec at a rate of 40Mbps)

- Includes 256 MB of RAM

- Has OpenGL ES2.0 and OpenVG library

- Has Secure Digital (SD card) sockets

- Can be powered through a 5V USB charger

- The original version came naked – it did not have a case for the printed circuit board

The RPi Model A features:

- HDMI and video outputs

- One (1) USB port

- SD card hole

- General purpose input/output Board connector

- Analog connector for 3.5 mm headphone jack

The RPi Model B features:

- HDMI and video outputs

- Two (2) USB ports

- SD card hole

- General purpose input/output Board connector

- Analog connector for 3.5 mm headphone jack

- 10/100 Fast Ethernet

The RPi Model B+ has the same features and specifications as the Model B, except it has four (4) USB ports.

Raspberry Pi is appealing to the public because it is affordable and is small in form. It is easy to hide and can be set up easily in an appropriate case. Most technology enthusiasts visualize the RPi as a secondary desktop – something that can be used for research and troubleshooting. Schools and businesses can install computers at very low costs. The RPi can also be used for niche applications.

The RPi is different from other small computer devices because its hardware is based on a closed source – the ARM SoC and a different GPU. Further, the intended use for the RPi is for it to be a final product – something that can operate on its own. Others are intended to be integrated in electronics or machines. Aside from the affordable price, the RPi also uses a non-modular design and boasts high clock speed and lower power usage. It is a device that is both competent and cheap.

Chapter 2:
Getting Started with your New Pi

This chapter details steps in setting up your Raspberry Pi:

You will need the following:

1. KEYBOARD AND MOUSE – You can use any typical keyboard and mouse for your RPi. A wireless keyboard and mouse can also be paired with your RPi.

2. DISPLAY AND CONNECTIVITY CABLES – Use an HDMI/DVI monitor and HDMI input cable. A TV will also work. For internet access, you will also need a standard Ethernet cable.

3. SD CARD - When you buy a Raspberry Pi, you get the full print circuit board. However, the package does not include an SD card. It is best to procure pre-loaded SD cards with updated NOOBS software. An 8GB class 4 SD card is highly recommended.

4. POWER SUPPLY – Like SD cards, the power supply does not come with your purchase. Get a 5V micro USB to power up your RPi. Do not use something with insufficient power – you need at least 700mA. The RPi may reboot if there is low ampage.

5. INTERNET CONNECTION – It is not really an essential but you can use the Internet to download or update your software.

6. AUDIO LEAD – For viewing videos or playing games, the standard 3.5mm jack earphones or headphones will suit your Raspberry Pi.

This is what you need to do:

1. PLUG IN YOUR RASPBERRY PI – After you secure the abovementioned equipment, you can now plug your RPi in. Do the following steps:

   a. Insert your SD card in the SD card slot. Make sure you do it the right way.

   b. Plug your keyboard and mouse into the USB slots

   c. Turn your monitor on and select the appropriate input (DV1 or HDMI1)

   d. Plug the Ethernet cable to the port to connect to the internet

   e. Plug the Micro USB power supply to turn your RPi on and boot it

2. INSTALL NOOBS (**N**-ew **O**-ut **O**-f the **B**-ox **S**-oftware)

   To select and configure your operating system, you need to follow the following guide:

   a. You can download NOOBS and install it on your SD card (8GB is the recommended size) or you can purchase one with pre-installed NOOBS.

      – To download, format your SD card first.

      – When your SD card is ready, use a computer and go to the Downloads page of the Raspberry Pi site. Click the NOOBS button with the download zip file. Save it on a selected folder.

- When you have finished downloading, you can safely remove your SD card from the computer and insert it in your RPi. You can then extract the files.

b. Initial Boot

- With everything ready and plugged in, you can boot your RPi. A window will come into view with a recommendation of various operating systems you can set-up and install. Raspbian is highly recommended.

- After selecting your OS, click INSTALL and wait for the installation process to be completed.

- Once installed, the configuration menu will load so you will be able to create user profiles and set the time and date. You can also enable the camera board.

- To exit the menu, click on TAB then FINISH.

3. LOG IN

Once you have successfully installed the OS, you will need to log-in.

If you used Raspbian, use the default login to get started.

Username: *pi*

Password: *raspberry*

You will see the following command line after a successful log-in: *promptpi@raspberrypi~$*.

As a security feature of Linux, you will not see anything on the screen when you type in the password. To access the graphical interface for user profiles, key in *startx* and press ENTER.

Chapter 3:
Raspberry Pi Tips and Tricks

Your Raspberry Pi can improve your computing skills and your programming knowledge. It is designed to make computing a practical proficiency. The command line is friendly instead of intimidating. Use the following hints to help you navigate the platform:

How to use TAB completion & command history

Writing a long command line or repeating it won't be a problem when you utilize the TAB completion and command history convenience of the Pi.

For example, you can type the first few characters of your command or file location then press the TAB key – the Pi will fill in the blanks and you can select the valid command or location you wish. Double tap the TAB key and you will reveal all possible selections.

On the other hand, the command history allows you to go back and locate the previous commands you have made. Press the UP key to view the commands and ENTER when you want to do a particular command again.

How to Copy and Paste

For your convenience, you can copy and paste bits and pieces of your codes or URLs. You need to highlight the text, right click and Copy. When you go to the terminal window, right click and Paste.

You can also use the short cut keys for Copy and Paste. Then add Shift: SHIFT + CTRL+v (or c). This tip is especially helpful when you are following an online guide and you need to copy a URL onto the command line.

How to install and remove software

You can install and remove software on the command line. If you have Raspbian, you have a bunch of amazing tools and applications in store. Get the APT to obtain it for you. To install the GNU Image Manipulation Program, for example, you just key in 'sudo apt-get install gimp'. When it isn't the application you want, you can remove it with this command: sudo apt-get remove gimp.

When you don't know a particular software name, you can use the APT search. Use the apt-cache search and you will have a result list on hand – with a description of each application. You can copy and paste the application in the install command.

If the selection is too much for you, you can pipe the results by using 'apt-cache search screenshot | less' to make it easy for you to scroll and search.

To see all the available software for your Raspberry pi in the open source, type 'apt-cache search . | less'. You will see a lot of Command Line Interface tools that you can interact with.

How to shut down your Raspberry Pi

Never just pull the power off your Pi because you can easily corrupt your file system. A corrupted system will mean lost files and you will need to install them all over again. You need to shut down your Pi using the command line. Type 'sudo shutdown -h 0'. It will make your Pi halt without any delay. Typing the following will also give you the same result:

- sudo shutdown -h now

- sudo poweroff

How to Reboot

You can reboot your Pi using the same shutdown command – 'sudo shutdown -r o'. You can also use 'sudo reboot now'.

How to open and edit files

You can utilize Nano – the text editor that comes with your Raspberry Pi.

Type 'nano' and the file name and location of the file you want to access.

To tweak the configuration file, key in 'sudo nano /boot/config.txt'. Use the arrow keys to scroll up and down, press CTRL+W and enter a search term. When you have finished editing, save the file by typing CTRL+O. Then press CTRL+x to exit to the command line.

Here are some more useful Nano commands:

CTRL+k - to delete an entire line

CTRL+d - to delete a character

CTRL+u - to undo previous command.

To make a new blank file, open it by keying in: nano my_new_file.txt. When you are done editing, press CTRL+x to exit. Press "y"+Enter to save your file. .

This will open a new blank file. Once you're finished adding and editing text simply press CTRL+x to quit – Nano will ask you if you want to save before you do (by pressing 'y' and Enter)

Chapter 4:
Raspberry Pi Projects

The RPi was initially designed for educational purposes – to learn new programming codes and perform common applications on a mini-scale. But there is so much more you can do with your Pi if you get creative enough. Some of the Pi projects may require a lot of time, effort and a few additional items but it will be worth it when you do complete them.

Here are a few projects you can experiment with your Raspberry Pi:

- Build a web browser

   You can hook your RPi up to a television and surf the internet on a big screen. Install Chromium as your browser for a better surfing experience.

- Make it a living room personal computer.

   Enjoy a media experience by utilizing OpenELEC. Simply hook your Pi to your TV.

- Play Minecraft

   You can enjoy the block-bashing game in mini-version on your Raspberry Pi for free.

- Build a digital garden

   Get a Pibrella board and some small motors. Make flowers and garden bees out of cards and other materials. Connect them with your Raspberry Pi and

Python 3 so you can have them moving and spinning at the touch of a button.

- Make Your Own Case

  Download a printable template, cut and glue it together to make a custom case for your Pi.

- Use Windows 3.0 on your Pi

  You can run Windows 3.0 and DOS 6.22 on your Pi using QEMU. Extract the VDI image from Kirsle then install QEMU.

- Robotics

  Explore robotics and create your own friendly robot. You can start with a robot butler using a Nintendo Wiimote and your Pi then attach a robot chassis and controller as you go along.

- Game Console or Arcade Pi Cabinet

  Bring your gaming level up another notch by creating your own arcade cabinet or retro game console. Customize an old cabinet and use programming codes to emulate a variety of gaming systems.

  Use RetroPie to emulate various consoles such as Mega Drive, Sega and NeoGeo. It will take you a while to install it but you will enjoy your classic games. Download some of these games for free.

  Raspberry Pi will automatically boot into EmulationStation and run RetroPie. Here is a list of other systems you can emulate:

- Amiga

- Arcade (PiFBA, ST/STE/TT/Falcon)

- Atari 800 and 2600

- Apple Macintosh (Basilisk II)

- Apple II (LinApple)

- Final Burn Alpha

- Game Boy Color and Advance

- C64 (VICE)

- CaveStory (NXEngine)

- Duke Nukem

- Doom (RetroArch)

- Game Gear (Osmose)

- Intellivision (RetroArch)

- MAME (RetroArch, AdvMAME)

- Sega Mega-CD, 32X and Master System

- Nintendo Entertainment System

- Playstation 1

- PC / x86 (rpix86)

- Z Machine emulator

- Scratch

  Children can learn the basics of programming by using Scratch.

- Servers

  You can utilize your Pi by making it a dedicated Torrent server or a cloud server.

- Morse code transmitter

  Get an old Morse code machine and mix it with your new Pi technology. Have fun programming, sending Morse code and decoding messages.

- Pi Cluster

  Make a cluster of Pis and build a supercomputer or media center.

- Stop-Motion

  You can set up a stop-motion-capable rig with your Raspberry Pi and a Pi camera by utilizing a few Lego mini figures, a breadboard, jumper wires and a tactile button. Take pictures using the tactile button that is connected to your Pi's GPIO pins through a Python code that you can use to control the trigger. Create custom movies and have fun.

- Wireless Access Point

  With the help of an SD care and a Wi-Fi dongle, you can use your Raspberry Pi to extend your Wi-Fi network's reach and connectivity. You can also set up a separate WiFi network.

- Point-and-shoot camera

You can build a point-and-shoot camera with your Raspberry Pi with a TFT screen. Some desoldering will be required.

- Car dashboard

You can use your Raspberry Pi as a touch-screen car dashboard to play music, browse through pictures and watch videos. The Pi is powered by the XMBC media center software so you can set up something that is highly functional and less expensive than off-the-shelf car dashboard screens. It may require a bit of time and effort but it is worth it in savings.

- Weather station

With a few pieces of additional hardware, you can use your Raspberry Pi to set up and power up your own weather station to get forecasts.

- Motion-sensing camera

With the help of a passive infrared sensor and some coding basics, you can capture some footage from your yard or home when you aren't there.

- High-alt balloon

Attach your Pi to a balloon to pick up images and videos from afar. You can have the images beamed back to you and you can track your Pi's location using GPS.

- Home automation

  Detect switches or pressure pads and automate your home by using PiFace.

Chapter 5:
Frequently Asked Questions and Troubleshooting Techniques

To enjoy your new Raspberry Pi, you may want to read up first on frequently asked questions and check out your manual so you can enjoy your Raspberry experience to its full potential.

1. What are Raspberry Pi dimensions?

    The Pi is roughly 85.60mm x 56mm x 21mm and weighs 45g. It is very compact. The connectors overlap over the edges.

2. How are the models A, B, and B+ different from each other?

    Model A – 1 USB port, 256 MB RAM, no network connection (no Ethernet port)

    Model B – 2 USB ports, 512MB RAM, with an Ethernet port.

    Model B+– 4 USB ports, 512MB RAM, with an Ethernet port.

3. What is the default username and password for my initial log-in with Raspberry Pi?

    Default username: pi

    Default password: raspberry

4. When I input my password, nothing happens. Why?

With a Linux OS, passwords are not displayed in the bash prompt. Don't fret that your keyboard is not working even if you don't see anything. Your Pi did not freeze.

5. I cannot find the on and off switch; where is it?

The Pi does not come with an on and off switch. You just plug it in to turn it on and you need to shut it down properly to turn it off. Remember to safely unplug your Raspberry pi so that you will not corrupt the system or re-image it.

6. What is NOOBS?

It means "New Out of Box Software". The NOOBS is an installation method that comes with your Pi.

7. Is the standard keyboard and mouse applicable? How do I connect them?

The Pi is compatible with standard keyboards and mice. All models have ports that can be used to attach any USB 2.0 device. You can utilize a USB hub.

8. What is a system-on-chip or SoC?

It is a system that includes all kinds of electronics such as CPU, USB, GPU, RAM, controller, etc. to make a computer run on a single chip. Your Raspberry Pi runs a Broadcom BCM2835 and is powered by an ARM1176JZFS that runs at 700Mhz.

9. Can I boot without an SD card?

No, you cannot boot if you don't use an SD card. The files are installed in the FAT32 partition so the Pi needs an SD card to initially boot.

10. Does the Pi come in self-assembly kits?

No. The Pi comes as finished boards and you cannot hand-solder kits.

11. How powerful is my Raspberry Pi?

The GPU is powered by Open GLES 2.0, hardware-accelerated with OpenVG, and a 1080p30 H.264 high-profile encode and decode. It is capable of general purpose computing, DMA infrastructure and texture filtering.

12. Is overclocking possible?

By default, Raspberry Pi runs at 700 MHz. You can overclock it by running 'sudo raspi-config'. However, you may experience stability issues as not every board can run at higher settings.

13. Does my Pi need a heatsink?

There is no need for a heatsink because the Pi does not become hot enough. There is no need for special cooling, like a cellphone.

14. Power Requirements

Raspberry Pi is initially powered by a 5-volt micro USB.

The current that you need to run applications is dependent the peripherals attached to it. A 1.2mA power supply can help you run most applications but you can also utilize a 2.5A if you want to use all four ports of your Model B+.

If you use peripherals that require more power, you must connect your Pi to a hub that is externally powered. This is because the various interfaces require different power requirements. For example, the GPIO pin will draw 16mA, the camera will use 250mA, the HDMI port will require 50mA and the keyboard and mouse may use 100mA to 1000mA.

15. Can I use a USB hub to power my Raspberry Pi?

Some hubs only provide 500mA per port, the Rapsberry Pi needs 700mA. There are other hubs that can provide as much power as needed per port. However, some hubs tend to back-feed the Pi and bypass the voltage protection. In cases of power surges, the Pi can be damaged.

16. Can I use batteries to run my Raspberry Pi?

If you run your pi directly off batteries, then you may end up damaging it. It will take extra special care in monitoring and maintaining this power source and you can only do this if you are an advanced user. To understand the complexity, consider that the 4 pieces of rechargeable AA batteries can provide 4.8v on a full charge. But if they lose their full charge, the system will become unstable. If you use non-rechargeable batteries, they will provide 6v of full charge which is beyond the tolerance range for your Raspberry Pi.

If you have a charger pack that can provide a steady output of 5v, then you can use it. Otherwise, it is best not to use batteries.

17. I am having power problems.

    To troubleshoot this, check the actual voltage on the circuit board. Remember to test the voltage when the Pi is not idle.

    Using a multimeter with a range of 20 volts DC, test the two points labeled TP1 and TP2. It should record a 4.75 to 5.25 volts. If it is lesser or greater, the problem is with the power cable.

    Here are the voltage concerns:

    Low voltage can mean that the power cable is not supplying enough current. You need t least 700mA in your power supply.

    Low voltage can also result from using a low quality micro USB power supply cable. They have thin conductors that causes voltage drops.

    When you have too many USB devices connected to your Pi, they use a lot of power. Raspberry Pi can only power up to 100mA of USB devices.

    You can also check if the F3 Polyfuse is bad or blown up.

18. Camera Information

    The Camera Board connects the CSI-2 camera port on your Raspberry Pi. A short ribbon cable allows a camera to be connected to capture still images and videos via the Image System Pipeline. The camera module is the same as that which is used for mobile phones, the Omnivision 5647.

The module can take photos of up to 5 megapixels (5MP) and record video with resolutions of up to 1080p30. It supports raw capturing and encoding in PNG, GIF, BMP and JPEG as well as uncompressed YUV and RGB photos. The videos are recorded as H.264, main, baseline or high-profile formats. You cannot use a camera module with more megapixels.

To use the camera, there are three possible command lines. One each for still images, videos, and uncompressed outputs. You can set the image sizes, exposure mode, compression quality and ISO just the same as compact cameras.

You can also extend the ribbon cable to up to 4 meters.

The camera board needs 250mA to function. Check that the power supply can provide enough power. You may need to remove other peripherals.

19. Video Information

You can use any of the following as a video display: analogue TV, digital TV, DVI monitor. Connect it through a cart connector or a composite. If you have a Model B+, you can use the 3.55mm composite jack which combines both audio and video. You will need an RCA adapter if you want to attach it to an older television. There is no VGA support so you need to use active adapters. Passive cables will not work.

Your Raspberry Pi can record and play H.264 (mp4/mkv). You can purchase additional codecs if you want to decode MPEG-2.

20. SD Cards and Storage

The minimum size of the SD card to use is the 6GB but the recommended size is 8GB, whether you use a NOOBS installer or a distro image. You need the free space to include packages and programs. You can connect a USB stick or hard drive of up to 32 GB for storage.

If you brick the Pi, you can restore it by re-flashing your SD card.

21. Networking, USB and wireless support

Raspberry Pi Model A does not support networking and wireless connectivity. The Model B and B+ have 10/100 wired Fast Ethernet built in. The Ethernet does not support Gigabit; it is attached via the USB bus.

There is no Wi-Fi built in Raspberry Pi models but you can use a USB Wi-Fi dongle.

You can use the hub to attach additional ports. Remember to use a powered hub.

22. Display Problems

When the startx fails to start or you get errors when you key in startx, you may be lacking storage space on your SD card.

The SD card may fill up with downloaded files in the 2GB main partition and you will only have a few MB of free space. Make sure that you free up some space and expand the partition.

You may have also incorrectly modified an .Xauthority file in your home directory. This will cause the startx to fail. You can fix this by temporarily moving, deleting or renaming the file.

When the screen has the wrong color, check the DVI cable. It should be screwed in properly.

When the video plays slowly or does not play at all, the problem may lie in the hardware-accelerated codec or the command line omxplayer. Use the command: *sudo omxplayer -o hdmi <path-to-filename>* to play .flv files.

When the composite displays black and white images only, you can edit the configuration file by adding the following command: *sdtv_mode=2*. The default composite display is NTSC output so you need to fix it.

23. Other General Troubleshooting Concerns

   o When you have the incorrect time

      Type the following in the command line to correct the time: *sudo dpkg-reconfigure tzdata*.

      You need to remember that Raspberry Pi does not have a real-time clock. It restarts counting from the last log in time. It needs to access a network timeserver to be updated. On other hand, the time can also be entered manually.

o   When a part breaks off

Some parts easily break off such as the silver
cylinder of the microUSB power input. It is a 220
uF capacitor that is prone to breaking off
because it sticks up and is mounted on a small
surface. You can solder it back on but be careful
to observe the correct polarity. The black stripe
should be connected to the board edge.

o   When you cannot install new software and you
see the error: package yyyy is not available, your
software is outdated. Get the latest software
available by using the following command: *sudo
apt-get update*. Then you can re-install the new
software. Make sure you install updated software
so you can continue using your RPi to its
optimum potential.

Chapter 6:
Get the Most Out of Your Slice of Pi(e)

Raspberry Pi is an amazing innovation in a small package. You can do so much with something so little. Now that you are enjoying your new Pi, you will be excited to explore the platform. You might want to learn some tricks and hack around with it.

Here are ten (10) cool hacks that may come in handy.

1. **Command line completion**

   This is one of the top favorite hacks to the Pi. When you want to do or look for something, you do not need to type out a long filename, command or path. It's what the name says: the command line is automatically completed for you as you type the first few letters of your action and press TAB. The command interpreter fills it in for you. Press TAB again and you will be shown a full list of possible commands that you can choose from. Select the appropriate one by pressing ENTER and the command code will run.

2. **Switch between terminal screens**

   You can use the ALT key with F1 to F6 so you can switch screens and multitask. It is fun to do especially when you are not using a graphical desktop.

3. **Go to the end or beginning of a command**

   It is easy to go from one end of a command to another. Key in CONTROL-A to go to the beginning and CONTROL-E to go to the end.

28

4. **Command history**

   Go to the command prompt and type a key. The command interpreter will show a cycle of your most current commands. You only need to press ENTER if you want to execute a particular command again.

5. **Take screenshots**

   If you need to take screenshots, you must first install scrot. This can be one by inputting the "*sudo apt-get install scrot*" command (without the quotation marks).

   Once installed, key in the command "scrot" in the terminal window. This will allow you to save a screen capture of the desktop in a PNG file. It will be saved in the working directory.

6. **Remote log-in**

   You can access your Raspberry Pi from another computer. To do this, key this in the prompt: *sudo raspi-config*. Then choose to enable SSH. Type *ifconfig* to access your Raspberry Pi's IP.

   If you are on a Windows computer, you need to use PUTTY. If you are using a Linux or OS X, key in "ssh pi @[ip address]" to log-in. (Remember to enter the command line without the quotation marks).

7. **raspberrypi.local**

   When you find it hard to remember your Pi's IP address, you should install *avahi-daemon*. Upon successful installation, avahi will bring you to the raspberrypi.local instead of your IP address.

8. **Access your computer's internet connection**

   You can share Wi-Fi internet connection via Ethernet from your computer to your Raspberry Pi.

9. **Create a Python web server with just one line**

   You can create a simple web server using Python so that you can access files in your working directory. You can even add an index.html file.

10. **sudo !!**

   You can execute a previous command as root when you type "sudo !!" (no quotation marks, space after *sudo* before the exclamation points) and you do not need to be a super-user to do so!

Have fun and enjoy exploring your Raspberry Pi!

Conclusion

Thank you again for downloading this book!

I hope this book was able to help you learn more about how to use your raspberry pi!

The next step is to put this information to use, and begin getting more out of your raspberry pi!

Finally, if you enjoyed this book, please take the time to share your thoughts and post a review on Amazon. It'd be greatly appreciated!

Thank you and good luck!